We Are All D

We All Move

Rebecca Rissman

Heinemann
LIBRARY

www.heinemannlibrary.co.uk

Visit our website to find out more information about Heinemann Library books.

To order:
☎ Phone 44 (0) 1865 888066
📄 Send a fax to 44 (0) 1865 314091
💻 Visit the Heinemann Bookshop at www.heinemannlibrary.co.uk to browse our catalogue and order online.

Heinemann Library is an imprint of Capstone Global Library Limited, a company incorporated in England and Wales having its registered office at 7 Pilgrim Street, London, EC4V 6LB – Registered company number: 6695582

Heinemann is a registered trademark of Pearson Education Limited, under licence to Capstone Global Library Limited

Edited by Rebecca Rissman, Charlotte Guillain and Catherine Veitch
Designed by Joanna Hinton-Malivoire
Picture research by Tracy Cummins
Production by Duncan Gilbert
Originated by Dot Gradations Ltd
Printed and bound in China by South China Printing Company Ltd

ISBN 978 0 431 19308 3 (hardback)
13 12 11 10 09
10 9 8 7 6 5 4 3 2 1

ISBN 978 0 431 19314 4 (paperback)
14 13 12 11 10
10 9 8 7 6 5 4 3 2 1

British Library Cataloguing in Publication Data
Rissman, Rebecca
We all move. - (We are all different)
1. People with disabilities - Orientation and mobility - Juvenile literature
305.9'08
A full catalogue record for this book is available from the British Library.

Acknowledgements
We would like to thank the following for permission to reproduce photographs: ©agefotostock p. **4** (Bigshots); ©drr.net pp. **8** (PAGE ONE), **16** (Ronald de Hommel), **20** (Stuart Freedman) **23 middle** (PAGE ONE); ©Getty Images pp. **6** (AFP/TEH ENG KOON), **7** (Patrick Byrd), **11** (China Photos), **12** (Brian Bahr), **14** (Doug Pensinger), **15** (Realistic Reflections), **21** (NBAE/Gergory Shamus), **22** (Amy Toensing), **23 bottom** (Brian Bahr); ©Jupiter Images pp. **18** (Marc Romanelli), **19** (Thinkstock Images), **23 middle** (Thinkstock Images); ©Landov p. **10** (REUTERS/Tony Gentile); ©shutterstock pp. **9** (dellison), **13** (Danny Warren), **17** (felix casio), **23 top** (dellison).

Cover photograph of Joshua Sundquist in the 2006 Turin Winter Paralympic Games reproduced with permission of ©drr.net (George S de Blonsky). Back cover photograph of a boy riding a specially adapted bicycle reproduced with permission of ©Realistic Reflections (Getty Images).

Every effort has been made to contact copyright holders of material reproduced in this book. Any omissions will be rectified in subsequent printings if notice is given to the publishers.

Contents

Differences

We are all different ages and sizes. We all have different coloured hair and skin. We are all good at different things.

How do we move?

People move in different ways.

Sometimes people move slowly.

People move to get to places.
Sometimes people move fast.

Ways we move

Some people run. Some people run on special blades.

Some people walk. Some people use a cane to walk.

Some people dance. Some people dance using a wheelchair.

Some people swim. People use
different parts of their body to swim.

Some people race. Some people race in wheelchairs.

Some people climb. Some people use ropes to help them climb.

Some people ski. Some people ski with special poles.

Some people ride bikes. Some people ride on special bikes.

Some people skip.

Some people swing.

Why do we move?

People move to keep fit.

People move to get stronger.

Some people move to have fun.

People move when they play.

We are all different

There are many different ways of moving. Which do you like best?

Words to know

cane pole some people use to walk

running blades special body parts made by humans. People use blades to help them run.

wheelchair chair with wheels. Some people use wheelchairs to get around.

Index

Note to parents and teachers

Before reading

Talk with children about the ways we are the same and different. Discuss how some of the differences are physical or mental and some are because different people like different things, but that all people are special and all people are equally important.

After reading

Encourage children to mind map different ways to move. Make a list of their suggestions on the board. Then go outside or in the hall and encourage the children to try each kind of movement, such as walking, running, hopping, spinning, crawling, or dancing. Play "Simon Says" with the children, giving them commands to move in different ways.